Calle

For Better or Worse

Tracey Morgan

Copyright © 2025 Tracey Morgan

ALL RIGHTS RESERVED. No part of this book may be reproduced, distributed, or stored in a retrieval system, or transmitted in any form or by any means, electronic, mechanical, photocopying, recording, or otherwise, without express written permission of the publisher/author. except in the case of reprints in the context of reviews, quotes, or references.

Unless otherwise indicated, all Scripture quotations are from the King James Version of the Bible.

Scripture quotations marked with NIV are taken from the Holy Bible: New International Version ®. NIV ®. Copyright © 1973, 1978, 1984 by International Bible Society. Used by permission of Zondervan Publishing House. All rights reserved.

Scripture quotations marked NKJV, are taken from The New King James Version. Copyright © 1982 by Thomas Nelson, Inc. All rights reserved.

ISBN: 9798304357487

Printed in the United States of America

Book cover, edits, and book were formatted by: Telleice Caraway

Nomakeupmonday.com

I want to take a moment to express my heartfelt gratitude to several individuals who have supported my husband and I with their patience and love:

First and foremost, I want to thank my husband of 41 years, Harold Morgan. He is the one God chose to be my life partner and to join me in fulfilling our mission on earth.

Next, I'd like to acknowledge my four wonderful children:

- Kaison, our eldest, who loves us unconditionally and always keeps us in his prayers.
- Prince, for his unwavering love and encouragement, which inspired me to write this book.
- Precious, for being a constant source of love and support, no matter the circumstances.
- Quinia, for her immense love and for meticulously typing and correcting my errors as I wrote my book.

I cherish you all dearly.

I also want to extend a special heart-filled gratitude to Pastor Derrick Crosby of New Fellowship Baptist Church for guiding us through our healing journey; God truly worked through him.

Last but not least. I want to send a special thanks to Apostle Robert Johnson of Real Life Church for teaching me about boundaries, which has been incredibly helpful. I am grateful for his wisdom.

Above all, I want to express my deepest thanks to my Lord and Savior, Jesus Christ, for choosing both of us. He entrusted us with this mission and the commitment to love each other through thick and thin. I love Him dearly. Thank you, Jesus.

TABLE OF *Contents*

Chapters

Introduction

I pray that every married couple who reads this book will find the strength to weather any storms they may be facing today. The intention is to infuriate the devil while standing firm on God's word. I pray for thriving, prosperous, healthy, and honest marriages between you and your partner. As you dive into this book, I hope you can learn from the trials and tribulations, as well as the mistakes my husband and I have experienced. My prayer is that through these pages, you will discover hope in knowing that God has the power to redeem and restore your marriage. I understand you might feel that your marriage is beyond repair given the challenges you're facing, but that's not the case. I'm here to remind you that nothing is too difficult for God! Nothing.... not addictions, pornography, dishonesty, strongholds, your past, or present. When a man and woman stand before God to witness their union, one of the vows they make is to support each other for better or worse. This moment marks the end of their single lives, bringing them together as one, so they are no longer regarded as two individuals but as one entity in the eyes of God.

The individual you marry on your wedding day is someone you believe you know well enough to potentially foresee your future together. This is where both the positive and negative aspects come into play. When we say "for better or worse," do we intend it solely for the wedding day, which is often considered one of the happiest moments in a marriage or can we genuinely uphold this promise during the challenging times that inevitably arise? Once you say, "I do," chaos often follows after the honeymoon phase. Have you ever wondered why that is? I have a response for you. The one thing the devil fears most is a thriving marriage. When you were single, he only had to focus on you, but once you united with your spouse, your mission grew in significance since you now had someone to stand with you when you go before the throne. Not only with you... but also on your behalf.

When two individuals unite for better or worse, with the Lord as their Savior, it becomes more challenging for the enemy to infiltrate their home and cause harm. However, my husband and I experienced a different situation. We were two young teenagers who became one and had no idea what becoming one was about. We had no idea what to expect, no idea about demons, generational curses, struggles, childhood trauma, and spirits that unknowingly clung to us. This lack of awareness made it easy for the enemy to invade and dismantle our home, doing everything possible to prevent our marriage from thriving as a kingdom marriage. Did the enemy win? Keep reading, and you'll discover the answer. I want to remind you that God only requires one person in a marriage to maintain a relationship with Him and uphold His Word, regardless of the circumstances. As you dive into this book, remember that God always has you on a mission, and your primary ministry starts at home.

Before diving into this book, take a moment to reflect on your marriage. Write about your feelings regarding both the joyful and challenging moments you've experienced together.

1 *Chapter* WE DON'T FIGHT AGAINST FLESH AND BLOOD

In marriage, we often attribute all negative experiences to the enemy and all positive ones to God. But what if we viewed every situation as something God has permitted?

When God allows events to unfold in your life, it enables Him to eliminate anything within you that does not reflect Him. For God to work through you, you must become more like Him, which starts with removing the influences you've allowed into your life and filling yourself with His presence. Once part of the enemy's Kingdom, you have now declared God as your Lord and Savior, and He is transforming you into a member of His kingdom. This transformation is challenging; we become so accustomed to our ways that we often don't recognize how they differ from God's nature. When God seeks to heal, restore, and deliver us, He must break us down before rebuilding us for His glory. Many battles arise, but the most significant one is the struggle within ourselves. We tend to engage in conflicts with our flesh, and every time we do, we find ourselves losing. The Bible reminds us, "We are not fighting against flesh and blood." This indicates that if we are not using God's Word in our battles, we are fighting ineffectively. This insight is crucial for your marriage.

When trying to lead your spouse towards Christ or help them see things from God's perspective, relying on your flesh will not lead them to salvation. Engaging in conflict with your spouse from a place of flesh rather than spirit will only drive them further away and signal a lack of trust in God. Understanding that your spouse's struggles are personal battles not against you. This will help you see that they are not your enemy. They were placed in your life because God believes you can fight for their spirit until they are liberated. The enemy is indifferent to a marriage that doesn't strive for the Kingdom, as it poses no threat to his domain. However, when you unite in Christ, your marriage becomes a formidable weapon against the enemy. This is when he will try to undermine your union; if he cannot tempt both partners, he will target the weaker one to turn them against God and your marriage. Remember, this is the moment to wield your spiritual weapon and engage in spiritual warfare rather than fighting each other. I learned this lesson early in my marriage: before I understood the power of praying in the spirit, I fought my husband in the flesh rather than with him or for him. This is our story.

As you dive into this book, you will encounter the vulnerable moments I've chosen to share, so you don't have to repeat the mistakes my husband and I made. I believe we had a tumultuous marriage, and if we could survive our darkest days, I am confident you can too. In Jeremiah 29:11, God tells us, "Before we were born, He knew us, and He has great plans for us as long as we surrender our lives to Him." Recognizing and believing that God can turn our struggles into good offers us hope. Having weathered the storms, we can now embrace the promises God has for our marriage that were written before we were born, allowing us to smile at the journey, knowing it has transformed us for the better.

When my husband and I united, we were not surrounded by married couples or positive role models. As teenagers, we stepped into this new chapter of life without guidance. When you are immersed in a particular way of living, you tend to adopt it. Both of us came from families that professed love for God, yet their lifestyles conveyed otherwise. This is how we approach our marriage, and when God isn't part of the equation, the enemy will surely take control. Many assume they know their spouse well enough to predict their future, but this often proves false. Challenges arise, and your spouse's reactions may differ from your expectations, leading to confusion and concern. You might start to question whether your spouse is who you thought they were or if they have changed. However, change is necessary for growth and should not be viewed negatively. We are called to fulfill the purpose God created us for, and our first ministry is within our homes. Marriage is a full-time ministry; what you invest in it will yield results. Prayer should be your battlefield, not verbal confrontations. Although I prayed for my husband daily, I often found myself arguing with him instead. I realized that my words were negating my prayers and obstructing God's work. As teenagers, we lacked the wisdom needed to confront the spiritual attacks against us, yet God had already mapped out our journey for better or worse. Keep tissues handy as you read our story; you may find parallels with your own experiences or recognize challenges you're currently facing. God has a plan for you, inviting you to walk in love and abundance.

Have you ever experienced a struggle within yourself? How did that situation unfold for you? What are some changes you can implement to help you focus on fighting in the spirit rather than in the flesh?

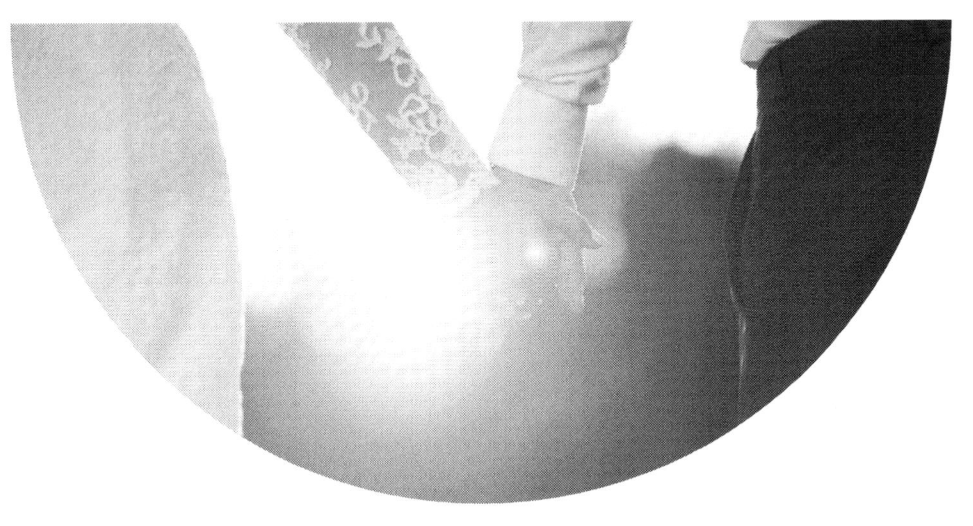

2 Chapter
THE GOOD, BAD, & UGLY

While the book identifies me as the Author, I genuinely believe that Jesus is the true writer of this story. Throughout the challenging times we've faced, I've often asked God how He would use our experiences for His glory, and this is where our journey begins.

Much of our story is filled with struggle, and I used to feel ashamed to share it because it was painful to endure. However, understanding that it all serves a purpose for God's glory makes me proud to tell it. This journey has allowed my husband and me to embrace our freedom, and I hope that as you read it, you too can find freedom and inspire others. We may think that our difficult stories are not useful to God, but the truth is that the more challenging the narrative, the more impossible it is for anyone to take credit for God's glory.

He has used so many ugly stories in the Bible, and here we are thinking things can be too ugly for God to use. Have you ever heard of Hosea in the Bible? I hadn't until one night, shortly after accepting Jesus Christ into my life, when I heard the name Hosea repeated in my dreams. That was the moment I discovered my purpose within my marriage; I had been unaware of how I arrived at my current situation, but it was all predestined for me to fulfill my calling. My calling initially frightened me; Hosea isn't typically a figure one would aspire to emulate. However, God chose me, and once He selects you, there's no escaping that path. It's encouraging to realize that when God calls you to fulfill your purpose, He has equipped you not only to navigate it but also to achieve victory.

Hosea was a prophet of God. He was called to marry a woman by the name of Gomar who was a whore. He was called to marry her even having the full knowledge of the fact of who she was. He was chosen to do this in order to demonstrate God's love. However, Hosea wasn't the only one being used by God. He used Gomer as well. However, for Hosea to fulfill his calling, it was essential for

Gomer to be in the right place at the appointed time when he discovered her. Gomer illustrates how we treat God, while Hosea reveals how God's love remains unwavering, regardless of our shortcomings. He tirelessly fights for us, no matter the circumstances. Let's be real: many women who experience infidelity often choose to walk away. However, I distinctly recall God conveying to me that I was meant to follow a different path, much like Hosea.

As I dived deeper into the book of Hosea and dedicated time to prayer and fasting, seeking clarity on God's calling for my life, I shifted my focus away from the negative aspects surrounding me. I began to concentrate on the positive outcomes that could arise from my situation. To achieve this, I had to remain steadfast in my calling rather than fixating on my present circumstances. Walking in God's perfect love proved to be a daunting challenge, especially since I wasn't receiving love from my husband. Nevertheless, I was enveloped in the ultimate love of God. When God calls you to a purpose, He not only equips you but also fills the emptiness, loneliness, heartache, and pain with His love, presence, and spirit, ensuring you are supported until your flesh aligns with your spirit.

The love I invested in my husband was not just for his liberation; it also drew me closer to God and affirmed that being a representation of Jesus Christ signifies His trust in me. Did it hurt? Absolutely. Did I sometimes feel like I was losing my mind for staying? Yes, indeed. Did I threaten to leave or feel inadequate at times? Yes, but only when I diverted my attention from God's calling on my life. The unconditional love I extended to my husband allowed him to grasp the essence of true love and motivated him to overcome alcohol, drugs, and infidelity. I felt called to love even during painful moments, facing judgment, enduring whispers about me, and confronting my own uncertainties. This reflects how Jesus loved us, fully aware that we would never be perfect or completely reciprocate His love. He recognized our imperfections yet chose to bestow His perfect love, hoping that we would eventually embrace Him. Many may deem my actions as foolish or irrational, but this calling was given to me by God, not by others. It was essential for me to resist allowing others to dictate my journey. When God calls you to a path, He equips you for it, making the journey easier for you, even if it appears daunting to others since it is not their calling. You are anointed for your unique purpose, not for your family or friends, so their opinions should not deter you from following God's plan for you. In the Bible, prophets faced severe consequences for disobeying God, often leading to death. Therefore, amidst all trials and tribulations, always prioritize obedience to God and strive to stay within His will.

What are some moments in your marriage that were good, bad, or ugly that you remember? Looking back on them and seeing where you are now, how does this shape your feelings about the calling that God has placed on your life?

3 *Chapter*

HE'S PREPARING YOU

When considering the concept of preparation, it's important to recognize that it is a process. Often, the steps involved in preparation may not be as aesthetically pleasing as the outcome we envision. From a spiritual perspective, God's preparation for us starts with His promises. He provides us with His word to rely on throughout this journey, as these promises sometimes do not happen overnight.

Many individuals spend their entire lives focusing on their present circumstances instead of holding onto God's promises. We have to remember the things God allowed in the Bible to happen to his people, but in the end, when they chose to stand on God's Word, they always walked out with victory.

In our daily discussions, my husband and I often reflect on the challenges and hardships we've encountered, acknowledging how God has used these experiences to prepare us for our journey. Despite the struggles we've faced in our marriage, God worked through the tumult to create something beautiful, even when we were unable to see it ourselves. In today's world, it's uncommon to find two people who stand by each other through every trial. We began our relationship when I was just 14 and he was 19, yet amidst all we endured, one thing remained constant: we always provided each other with unwavering support.

At times, we seek God's assistance in stepping into our destiny, unaware that we have been on that path all along. This is why God emphasizes that when we look after others, He will ensure our needs are met. It's His way of reminding us not to focus solely on our current situation, but to persist in the work He has entrusted to us. In doing so, we will eventually recognize how He has been guiding us through our challenges. God used Hosea to love a whore. People may question why God would allow him to endure such challenges. Do you think Hosea felt good loving a woman that he knew was a whore? I don't think he did, but he permitted God to work through him by embodying love, regardless of Gomer's present circumstances. This is the love that God has destined for my marriage. Although it has been the most challenging journey of my life, it has guided me toward my purpose and equipped us for our future. While it may sound beautiful, there were moments when God revealed my husband's actions to me through dreams. He couldn't refute them because he understood that I would never misrepresent the Holy Spirit. Before I could share what I already understood, he would enter the house with an attitude, perceiving that I was throwing things and expressing all my pent-up anger. There were times when I felt a deep urge to hurt him, even to the point of wanting to kill him, due to the pain he caused. Being saved doesn't erase the wounds; it doesn't define one's humanity. In a marriage, your partner's actions can deeply affect you. I have approached God many times, expressing my frustration and my inability to handle this situation on my own. It was then that He reminded me that if I allow Him to dwell within me, I can embody His presence on Earth. He doesn't expect us to be flawless; rather, He wants us to seek Him in every challenge and hardship we face.

This journey is not one that just anyone can undertake; God specifically selects those He knows will surrender themselves to Him for His glory. It's not about our desires if we wish to reach Heaven; it's about His will being done on Earth as it is in Heaven. There was a time when God allowed me to divorce my husband due to the choices he made, but He also told me that if I stayed, I would witness his soul being saved. He is not only my husband and the father of my children but also a soul that God deemed worthy of the struggle. The cost was significant, yet it was paid through Jesus

Christ, who chose to use me to guide him toward his freedom. When we fully commit ourselves to Jesus Christ, we begin to realize that our suffering pales in comparison to the pain He endured on the cross for all of us; after all, He was perfect, and we are not. Whenever I found myself expressing to God that the pain was too much to bear, He would remind me of the burden He carried for me. I want to encourage every spouse: standing in the gap for your partner will bring immense pain, but if you remember that God has equipped you for this moment, you will grasp your purpose and not dwell on your suffering. We all aspire to enter the Kingdom, but we must first fulfill our earthly responsibilities before hearing Him say, "Well done."

Have you recognized what God is preparing you for? If so, what insights have you gained from the experiences God has allowed in your life that aid in your preparation?

4 Chapter
LET HIS WILL BE DONE

Regardless of the challenges we face in life, our ultimate desire should always be for God's will to prevail at the end of each day. Husbands and wives must recognize that when they marry, promising to stand by each other through thick and thin, the nature of those challenges is unpredictable.

Supporting a struggling spouse requires sacrifice; and as anyone who understands sacrifice knows, it often comes with discomfort. In my marriage, fulfilling God's will meant standing by my husband and demonstrating the boundless love that God offers us. This love not only brought my husband closer to me but also drew him nearer to God.

If you are in a marriage, remember that God has equipped you with everything you need to navigate it successfully together. This journey won't be easy, and only the strong will endure. Expect daily challenges as two individuals unite as one. To ensure God's will is accomplished, rely on spiritual strength rather than your own power. Victory comes through fasting, prayer, and unwavering faith in your petitions. Engage deeply with the Word of God, allowing it to transform you from within.

Each day, you may wake up to new threats against your marriage, with the devil as your primary adversary. He will do everything in his power to deter you when you commit to pursuing fulfillment in your relationship. Hell is disturbed by your dedication to your Father's mission, prompting it to target the most vulnerable aspects of your life. If the enemy sees you pleading for God's intervention for your spouse, he may try to use your partner against you. Yet, you must remain steadfast in God's promises, regardless of how dire the situation may seem. Trust that God can fulfill His Word.
Allow the power of Christ's sacrifice to fight on your behalf, and remember to avoid battles in the flesh. You have been equipped for the journey God has set before you. If He was able to work miracles

for two teenagers, He can certainly do the same for you and your spouse.

Do you find it challenging to wait for God's will to unfold? During this waiting period, what activities do you engage in while anticipating the fulfillment of His promises? Have you ever experienced a moment when you didn't wait on God, resulting in less than the best outcome?

5 Chapter

DON'T ALLOW THE TEMPORARY TO BECOME PERMANENT

Before truly uniting with someone, several factors must be considered. While love is undoubtedly a significant element, what happens when fatigue sets in and you find yourself unwilling to love your partner due to a temporary circumstance?

Divorce often appears to be the simplest solution, and many choose this path when their current situation seems to outweigh their feelings for one another. I'm not generalizing all divorces, but it seems that few are genuinely fighting for love these days. In our modern society, many individuals strive for immediate gratification, and when they no longer desire what they have, they replace it as if it holds no value.

It's crucial to ask the right questions before becoming one with another person, but it's their actions that truly matter. Many claim to have a relationship with God yet spend little time nurturing it. People often know how to present themselves appealingly until they achieve their desires. My husband, for instance, was the most romantic young man I had ever met, showering me with roses and affection. This attention blinded me to many behaviors I should have scrutinized. To be honest, we were both young and had low standards. Growing up in homes without fathers, we watched our mothers work tirelessly to support us. Surrounded by broken families, we fell in love with each other's struggles, hoping to find rescue in one another. Have you ever found yourself attracted to someone because you recognize your own brokenness in them? Do you think, "Since we are facing similar challenges, it must be God's plan?" My question is, if both of you are sinking, who will support you? The day I chose to commit my life to Christ, I was desperate and weary of living like those around me, only to end up in the same place. How can your marriage endure? Don't wait until after the wedding to tackle difficult topics together; you'll want to see how your partner handles pressure and challenging circumstances.

This insight reveals their true character and who they turn to in times of trouble. I didn't have those crucial conversations with my husband before we married; I was an excited teenager convinced we were ready, thinking marriage only meant enjoying the good times and avoiding the bad. If only we had someone to guide us on what marriage really entails and how to truly understand each other.

Some essential questions to discuss include:

- *What is your relationship like with your parents?*
- *Do you have a relationship with God?*
- *Do you have children?*
- *How many sexual partners have you had?*

These inquiries help you understand the life experiences they bring into the marriage. While my husband was my first sexual partner, he had previous experiences, which shaped our journey. It's crucial to engage in conversations about the topics that make you uncomfortable; these are often the ones that need to be addressed. Temporary happiness and challenges can either strengthen your bond or create rifts that push you apart. Remember, everything is transient. When difficulties arise, view them as opportunities for growth together, rather than allowing them to burden your relationship to the point where you believe separation is better. At a young age, we were determined to navigate life together, but our choices also attracted various influences into our marriage. Moreover, there is a cost to committing to a lasting relationship, but if God has united you in marriage, know that you have the strength to face challenges together.

Are you familiar with the complete concept of the Armor of God? Start by reading Ephesians 6:11-18 and make it a daily practice to pray this over your marriage. Imagine how your life might change if you devoted as much time to prayer as you do discussing your challenges.

6 Chapter
DON'T TAKE IT PERSONAL

Proverbs 18:22 tells us, "He who finds a wife finds a good thing and obtains favor from the Lord." When my husband and I came together, I never imagined I would become a prayer warrior; I was the complete opposite of who I am now —shy and hesitant to speak up. However, everything shifted when God began to guide me into my purpose.

Today, if you ask my husband, he will tell you that without my prayers, he wouldn't have found the protection he needed during a challenging time when he was lost in his own desires. We should be partners who remain steadfast when our spouse deviates from their course; after all, marriage is about being there for one another through both challenges and triumphs. Marrying someone means committing not just for the joyful moments, but also trusting that this person will stand by you during your toughest times.

The most significant lesson I learned while my husband battled his addictions was to avoid taking his struggles personally. What do I mean by that? When someone engages in adultery or grapples with addiction, it often stems from their internal battles, not their partner. Whenever he acted in ways that hurt me, it impacted him even more deeply because he was fighting his own demons. Am I excusing his behavior? No, but as I delved into God's Word, I realized that we often let our feelings cloud our understanding of what God wants us to hold onto. God transformed my perspective in marriage, allowing me to see my husband not just as my spouse, but as a lost soul in need of someone to intercede for him. While I stood in the gap for him, God was intentional in sending people into my life to pray for my strength, guiding me through the journey He had laid out for my marriage.

Even with support, I found myself attempting to resolve issues independently. I realized that no amount of love, time, or attention could address the deeper struggles my husband faced. I needed to learn to genuinely trust God and take a step back. Your experience may be different, and your partner may be facing distinct challenges, but the essence of the journey remains unchanged. Pray for your spouse during their difficulties and allow God to unveil His promises for your marriage. The enemy seeks to create division, hindering you from achieving the Kingdom marriage that God has envisioned for you. Always remember, we are called to guide souls to Christ, and it all begins at home.

I was the one in our marriage God called to operate as Hosea or as a child of God, which means what my husband did or didn't do could not change my calling. In Hosea chapter 1 verse 2, it states, "And the Lord said to Hosea, go, take unto thee a wife of whoredoms and children of whoredoms and marry her." Hosea's calling wasn't easy, Hosea's calling didn't feel good. Hosea's calling looked foolish to people, but Hosea knew it was what God called him to. God didn't just give Hosea a calling, but he gave him a promise to look forward to as long as he didn't give up. Hosea was a righteous man, and God's assignment was for him to marry a whore because God wanted to demonstrate his love to his people, and he also knew he could trust Hosea to love her in the way God does.

Did you know that God places trust in you regarding your spouse? Many individuals enter marriage with a selfish perspective, but it's essential to recognize that your spouse's struggles are not theirs alone; they are also yours to share. Hosea interceded for Gomer, the transformation didn't occur instantly; it required his persistent prayer and faith in God's promise. Despite her ongoing battle with addiction, he remained steadfast in his commitment to love her unconditionally.

There were countless nights when I questioned whether I had truly heard God, as things didn't unfold according to my timeline, and I felt I could not persevere any longer. Throughout these twenty years of fighting for my husband's salvation, God consistently provided me with what I needed. Each person's timing and journey are unique, but we endure these trials to assist others. Writing this book is my way of guiding both single and married couples to understand that what God is calling you to do on Earth is what He has already equipped you for, and He trusts that you will fulfill that purpose.

Have you ever experienced the tendency to take things personally in your relationships when someone hurts you? As you move forward, I encourage you to concentrate on the choice that person made and offer your prayers for them instead of internalizing the hurt. Frequently, that individual may be dealing with their own challenges and may not mean to inflict pain on you. Take a moment to jot down the names of those for whom you can pray, and consider strategies to help you avoid personalizing their actions.

7 *Chapter* WHILE YOU WAIT

Take a moment to reflect on your life and consider what God has entrusted to you. This is the aspect of your life that draws you closer to Him, even if others question your choices. It is in this space that God intends to use you, leading you to seek His presence daily because you recognize your own limitations.

Often, the very area in your life where you are praying for healing and restoration is the one where God wants you to invest in others. I recall numerous times when spouses reached out for prayer, grappling with potential divorce, infidelity, or seeking freedom from their struggles. We would pray and fast for their spouses, and soon I would receive calls filled with testimonies of how God was intervening in their situations. Meanwhile, I was facing similar challenges in my own marriage. This left me perplexed—how could I be praying for others but not experiencing the same resolution in my own relationship? I witnessed many prayers being answered while I continued to wait.

In my waiting, I watched others receive what I longed for, which was painful. It felt at times as if God was indifferent to my predicament, but I realized my perspective was skewed. God cares deeply for me; He assured me that while I wait, He will use my pain to support many marriages struggling to find their path. As I embraced this understanding, my focus shifted from what I was lacking to what I could learn and share. My waiting was not wasted; it was a season of deepening faith and resilience. God will work through you during your waiting period, but it's essential to place your trust in Him rather than your pain. Pain can be so overwhelming that it may lead you to believe there's no escape and that this is the conclusion of your story, but that's exactly what the enemy wants you to think. In your waiting, engage in worship. Pray and fast. Surround yourself with like-minded individuals. Delve into God's Word, stand firm on it, and have faith in His promises. While you wait, God is preparing you and addressing what needs to be transformed within you to fulfill the desires you've been longing for. Shift your focus away from the waiting, and concentrate on what God is preparing you for; His promises will always come to fruition. So, from this moment forward, view your waiting as a positive sign from God that it's simply not your time yet, but rest assured, you are not forgotten.

How do you usually spend your time while anticipating God's promises? Have these actions been beneficial in the past? Reflect on activities that can support your spiritual growth during the waiting period, jot them down, and commit to them; remember, consistency is essential.

8 *Chapter* HOLD ON TO GOD'S PROMISES

Through all my trials and challenges, the most profound reward has been witnessing the fulfillment of God's promises. As a young girl, I yearned to feel wanted, loved, safe, cherished, and accepted. I believed that marrying as a teenager would alleviate those concerns, but I soon realized I was mistaken.

Jesus provided me with everything I sought, allowing me to release my husband from the expectations that only God could meet. Often, we focus on the allure of material promises, yet during my struggles, what God has truly given me is the assurance of His presence. Today, when I look in the mirror, I can genuinely say that I love myself. I am living in the reality of God's promises, and I am immensely grateful to witness the fulfillment of His promises within my marriage. If I had lost faith in what God entrusted to me, I would have missed out on the countless blessings He has showered upon me and my marriage.

Choosing to give up would have been much more difficult than persevering because it would have left me feeling disconnected from my divine purpose. Everything we experience is temporary, but our actions for the Lord and our obedience to Him are what ultimately lead us to the kingdom of our Savior. After all, the goal is to reach Heaven. When I reflect on my marriage, I can see Jesus present in every season, as He has transformed our struggles into blessings. This journey would have been unachievable without my deep love for Jesus; I have wholeheartedly committed myself to Him and genuinely desire to embrace the plans He has for me. I continue to walk in my calling, anticipating wonderful things to come, and in the meantime, I choose to share my story to inspire others. Marriage is a beautiful journey, even amid our toughest moments, because it allows God to fulfill His purpose in our lives. As I encourage you, these are the words I wish I had during the challenging times in my marriage. Your life is predestined (Ephesians 1:5), which means that before you were even born, God had already mapped out your entire journey on Earth. Everything that has occurred in your past, what you are experiencing now, and what lies ahead has been preordained, and no one can alter that. Take comfort in knowing that if you follow Him, God's promises for your life will come to fruition. Always remember to take a breath and seek His presence each day; in that space, you will find the strength to keep moving forward. Most days will be difficult, but those are the moments when God is urging you to draw closer to Him because He is nurturing what you need for your future. My husband and I's story is still unfolding, and so is yours. After 41 years of marriage, He is still working with us, and as we continue to trust God on our journey, we have learned to keep our focus on Him. Always remember to turn to God rather than people; it is God who called you to this path, not your loved ones or friends. We are all called to love, for better or worse.

Are you aware of God's promises for your life and marriage? If you're unsure, take some time to pray and fast about it. Once you have clarity, make sure to write them down here. This will serve as a reminder of the blessings that await you.

About Me!

Morgantracey43@gmail.com
Facebook: Tracey Morgan

As a child, Tracey aspired to become a nurse, and although she graduated from nursing school, she ultimately chose not to pursue a career in that field. She realized that her desire to be a nurse stemmed from her admiration for her mother's profession.

At a young age, Tracey married her husband, Harold Morgan, on November 10, 1983. Together, they raised four wonderful children: Kaison, Prince, Precious, Quinia, and a stepchild, Jamel, whom she loves as her own. Following the tragic events of 9/11, Tracey and Harold relocated to Mississippi. They had operated a cleaning service just a few buildings away from where the planes struck. Leaving New York City was a decision Tracey never anticipated, but it turned out to be one of her best decisions. In Mississippi, she discovered her true purpose and gifts.

Tracey has a deep love for prayer, a gift she cherishes. For the past 14 years, she has committed to a prayer line that meets Monday through Friday at 7 a.m. She has always been open to being a vessel for God's work. Additionally, she leads a ministry called "For God's Glory," where she and her family provide meals for the homeless- one of her greatest passions. Beyond feeding the less fortunate, she also loves to uplift and encourage women in the faith. From 2014 until she began her ministry in 2019, Tracey served as the chaplain at the Forrest County Jail. Tracey and her husband have owned "Omni Cleaning," a business, of eight years, offering services in various capacities. She lives a life dedicated to fulfilling God's calling, finding joy in praying and interceding for marriages. Known for her selflessness, Tracey Morgan exemplifies love through her faith and her actions.

Monday- Friday 7am

+667-770-1057

Access code: 895231

Weddings rings on bible by: Pexels from Pixabay -pg 8

Young wedding couple by: Halfpoint - pg 15

Getting married-matrimony by: Getty Images -pg 22

Praise the Lord by: Getty Images -pg 29

Wedding rings on wood by: Nicolas Trezeguet from Getty Images Pro -pg 35

Strand Liebe by: Getty Images - pg 41

Wedding rings on a bible by: Soup Stock - pg 49

Tomb of Jesus Christ with a cross by: Photocreo - pg 55

Canva Pro was used for all pics

Made in the USA
Columbia, SC
19 June 2025

59638136R00041